THIS JOURNAL

Belongs to

....

"Where words fail, music speaks"

Hans Christian Andersen

Cover and interior design by Sherry Frewerd

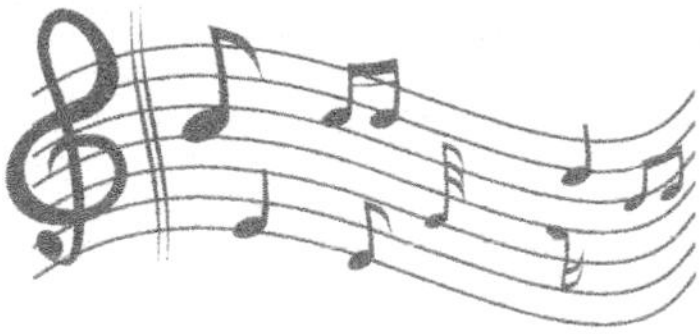

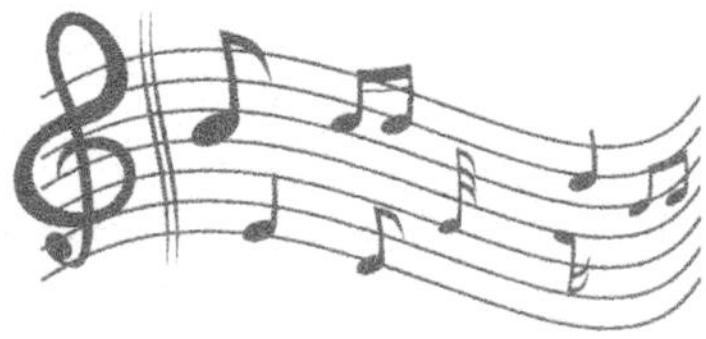

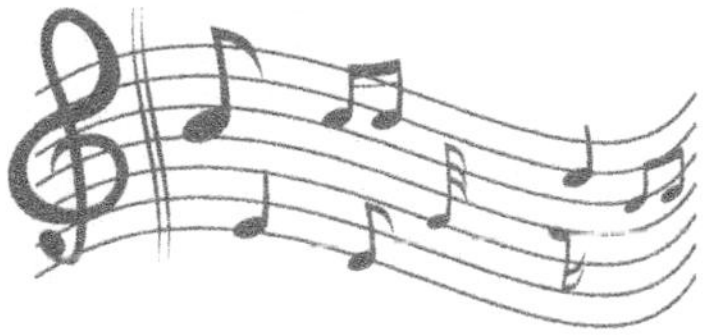

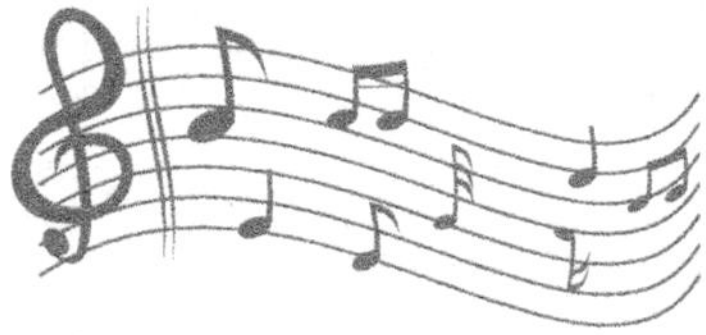

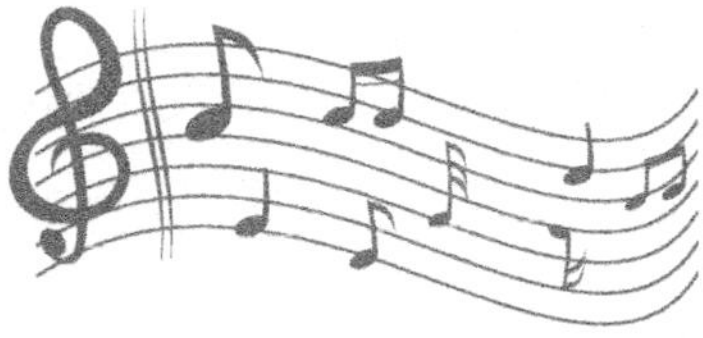

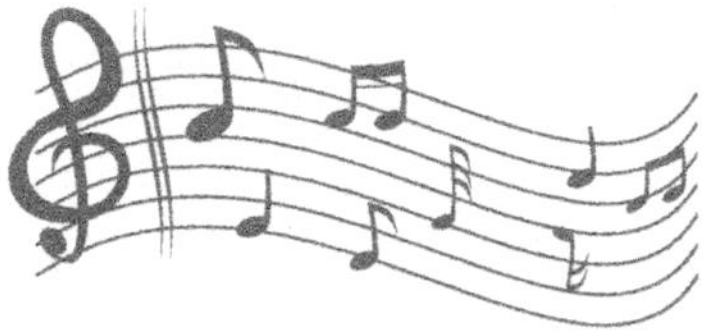

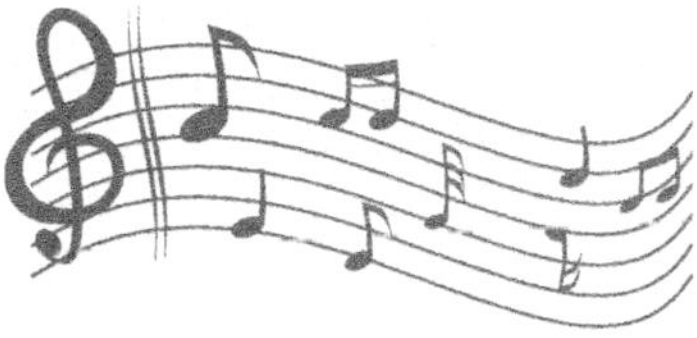

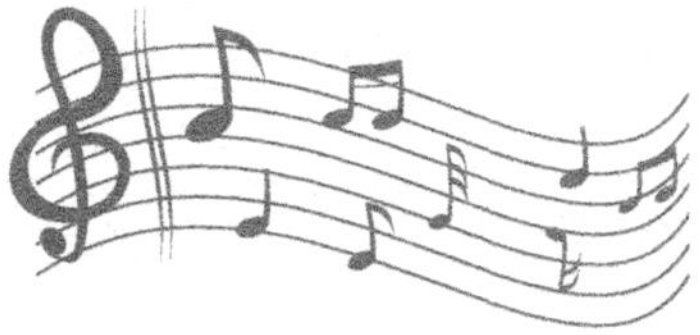

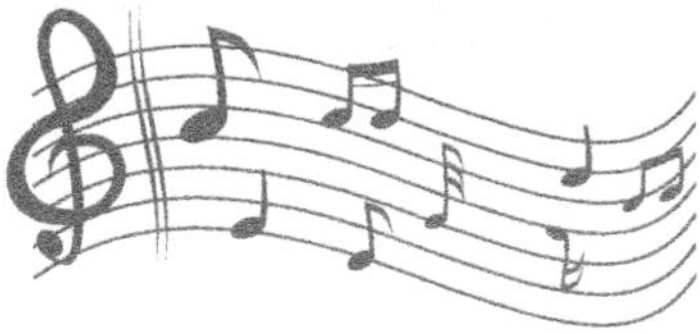

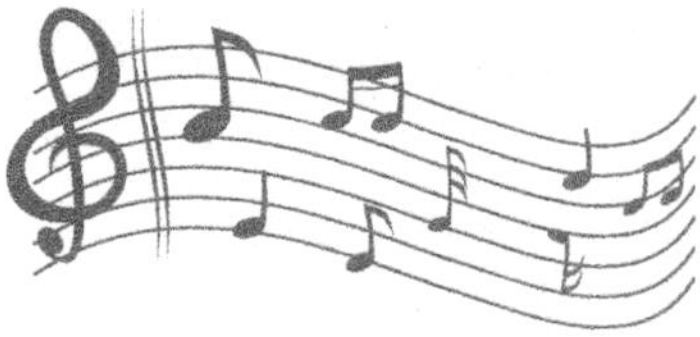

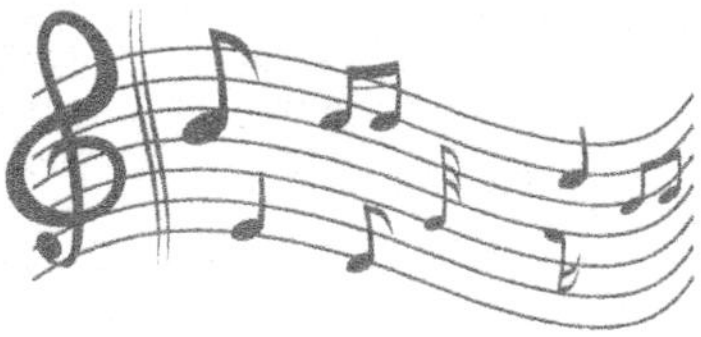

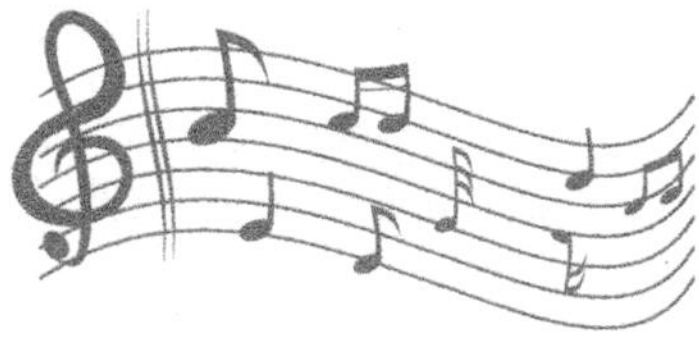

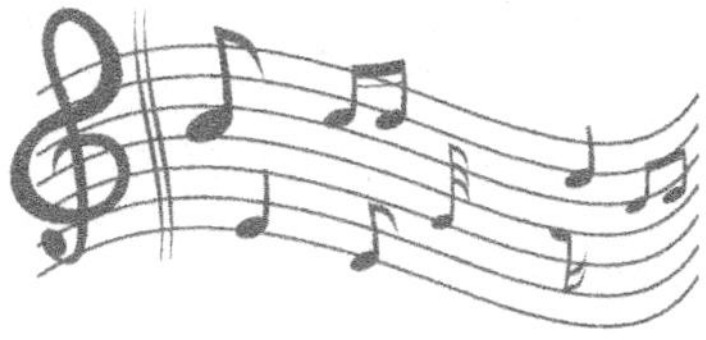

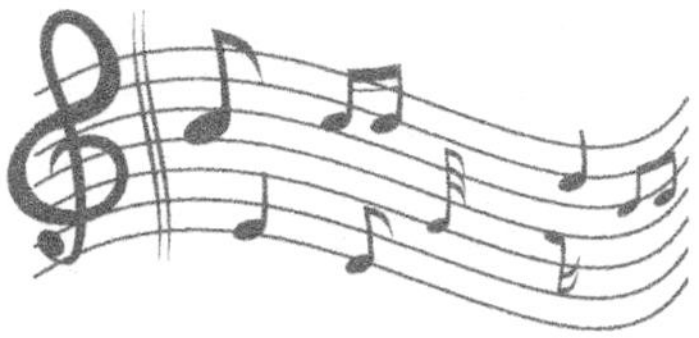

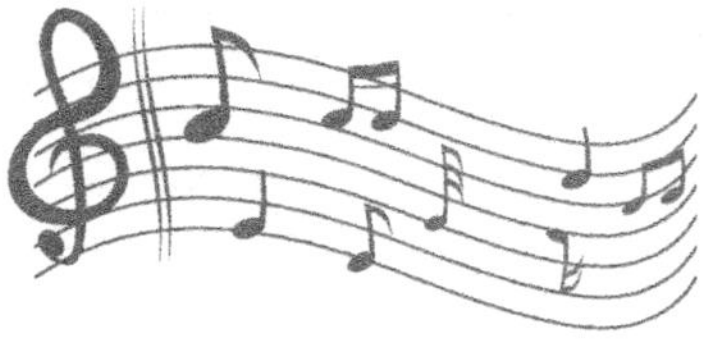

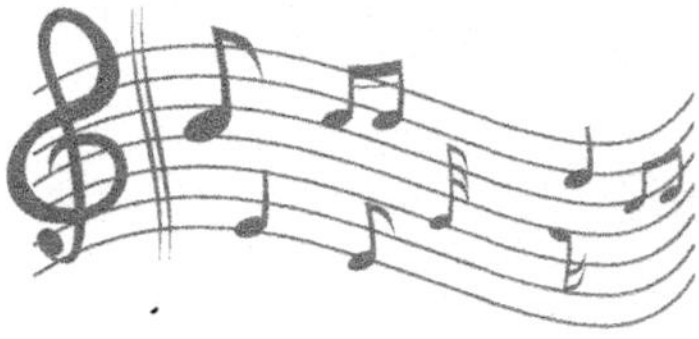

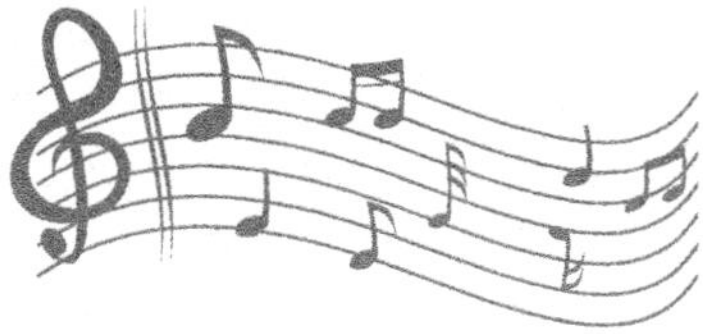

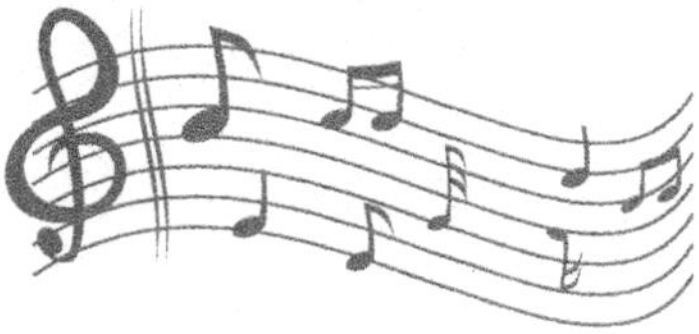

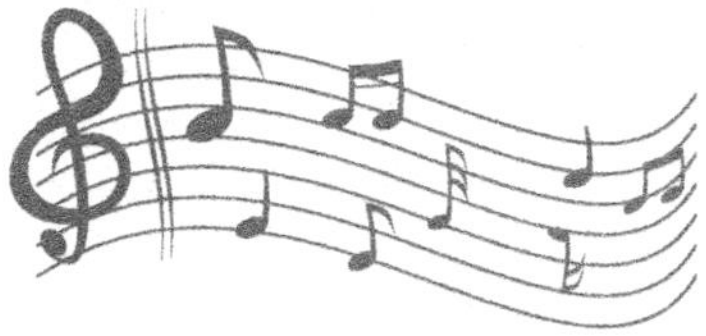

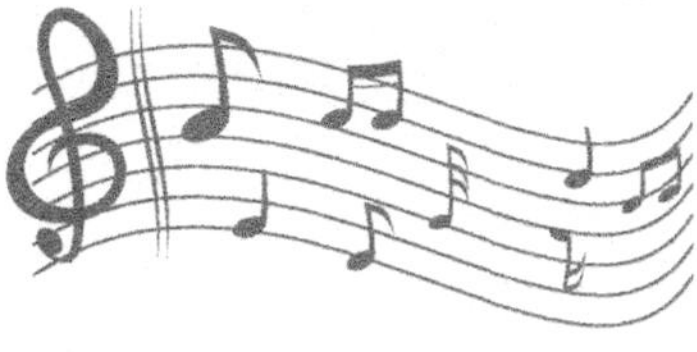

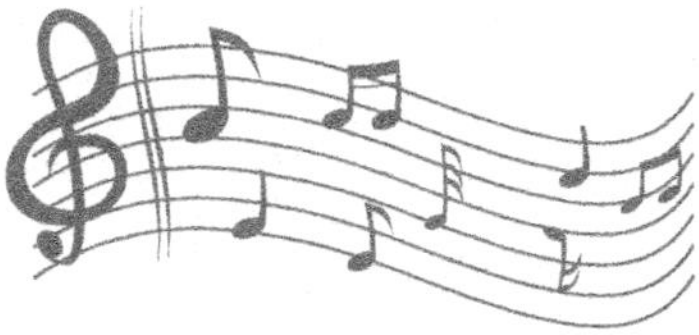

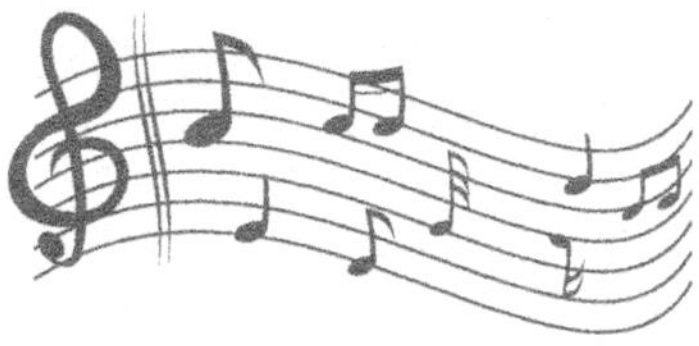

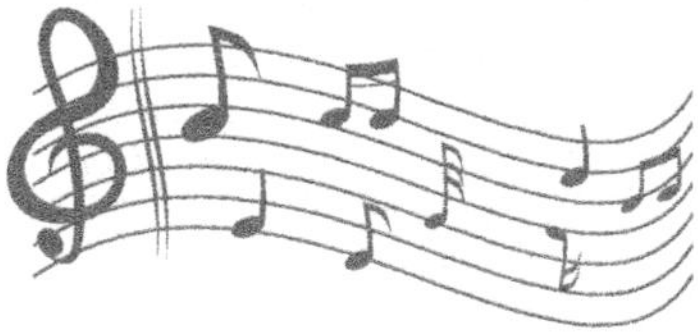

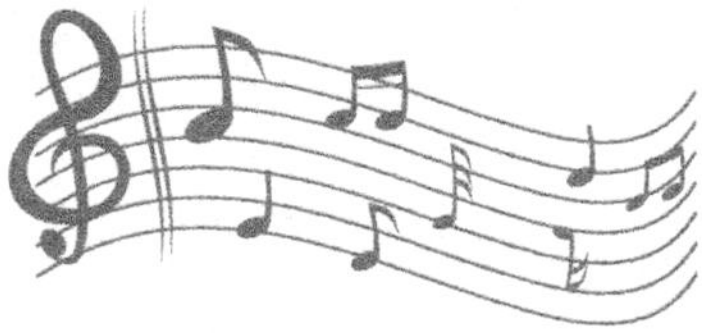

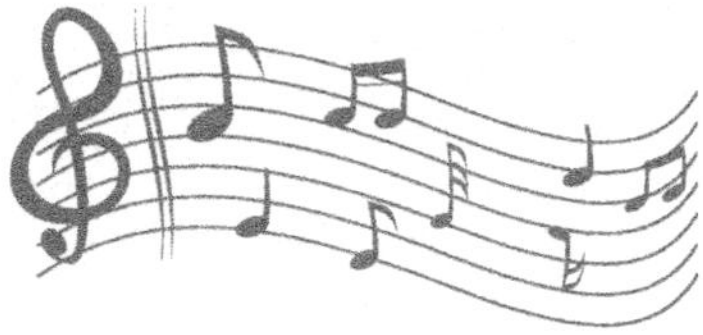

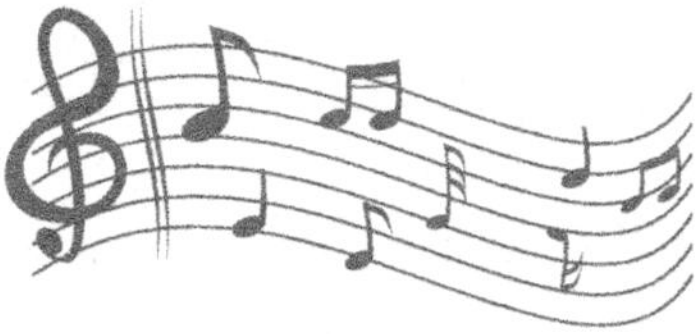

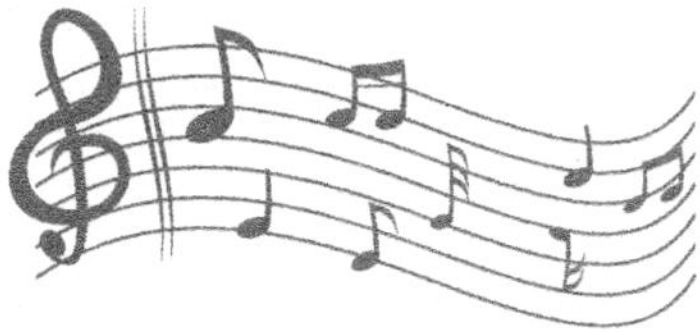

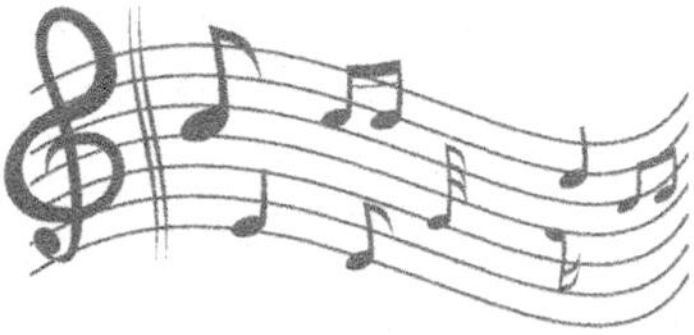

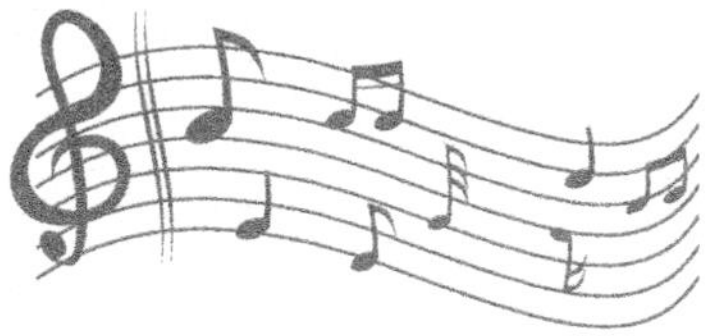

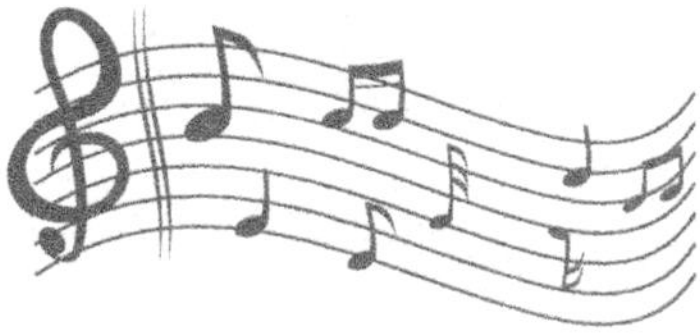

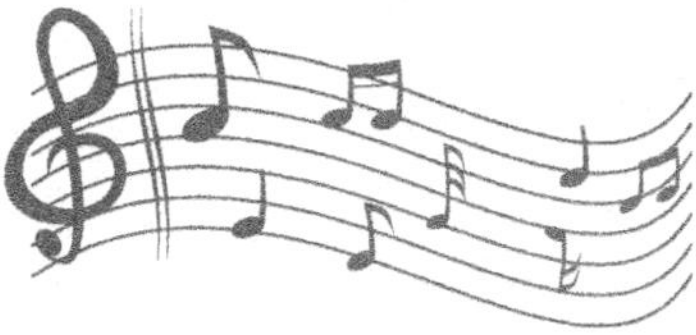

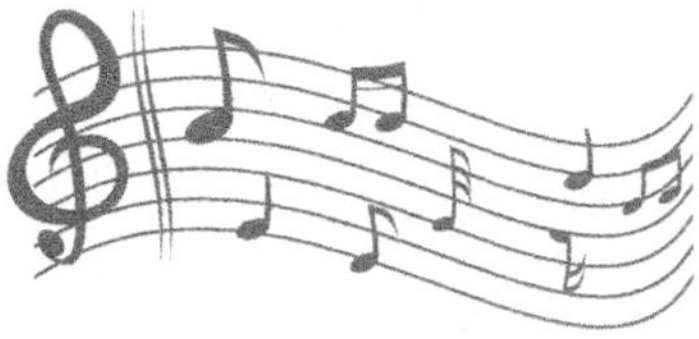

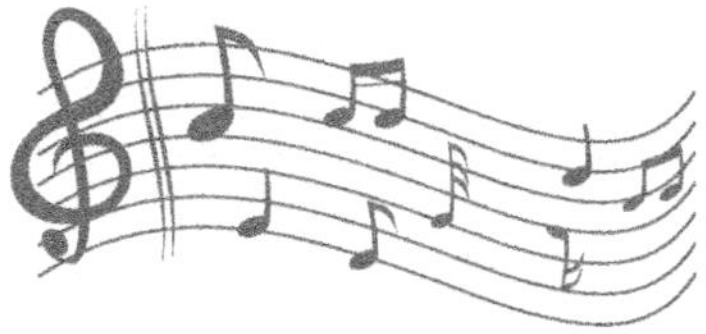

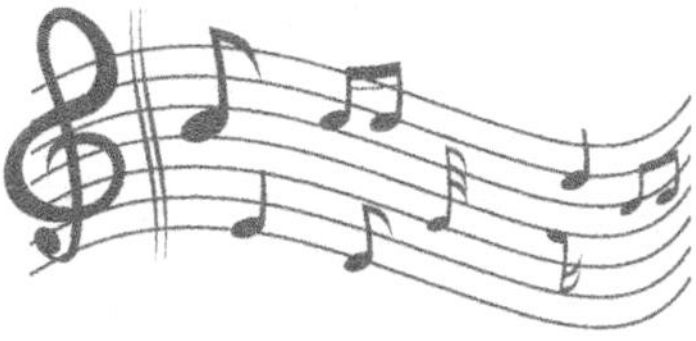

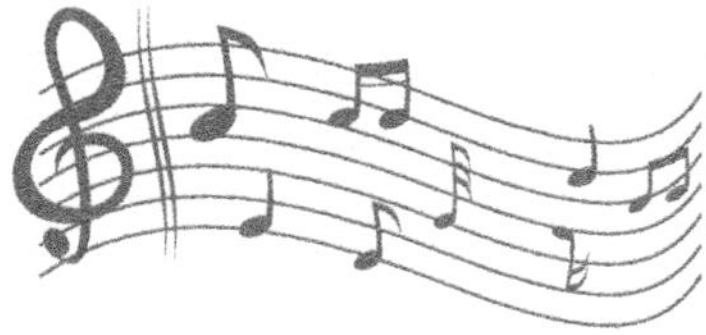

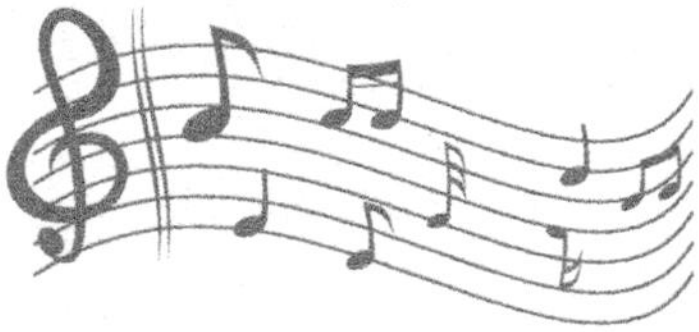

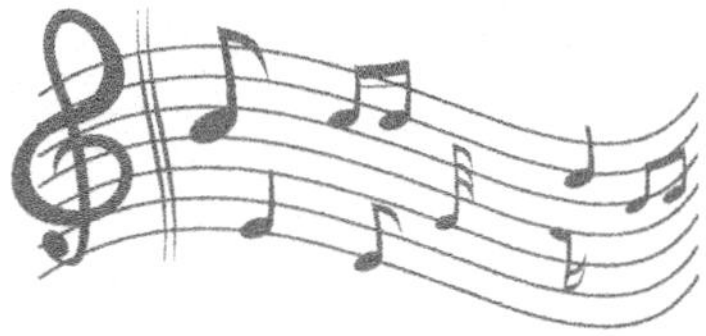

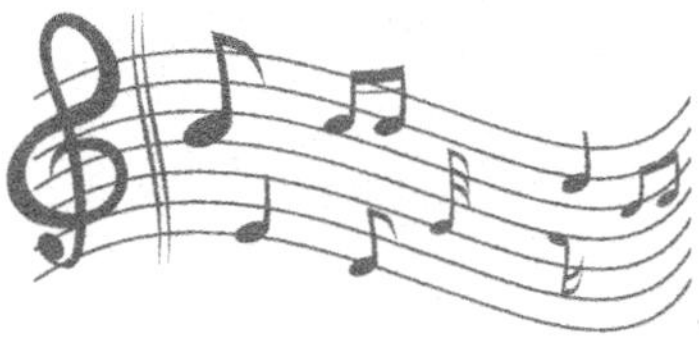

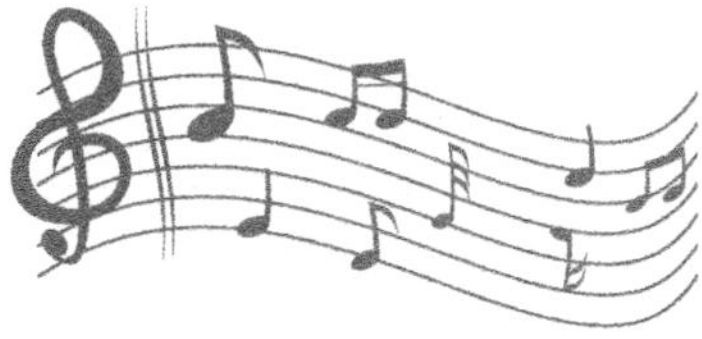

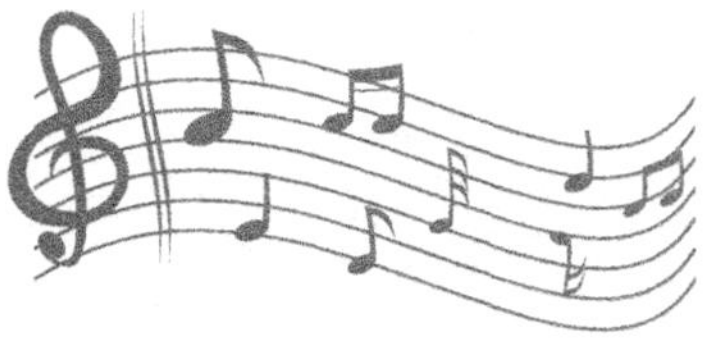

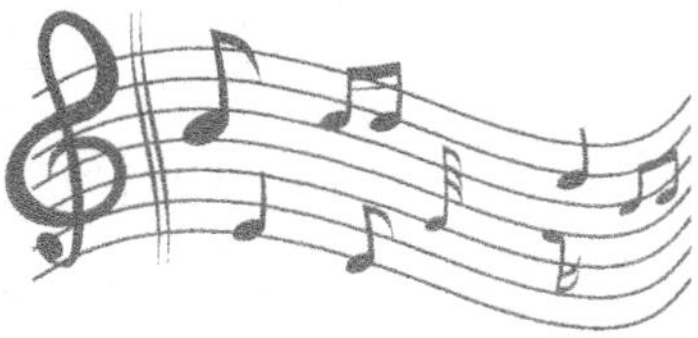

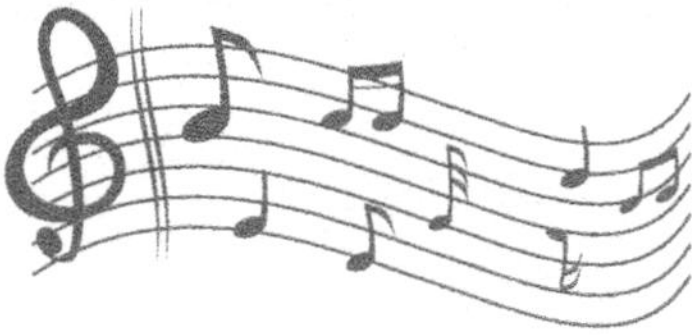

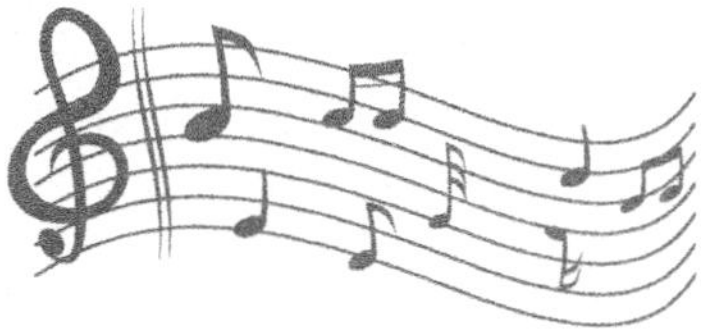

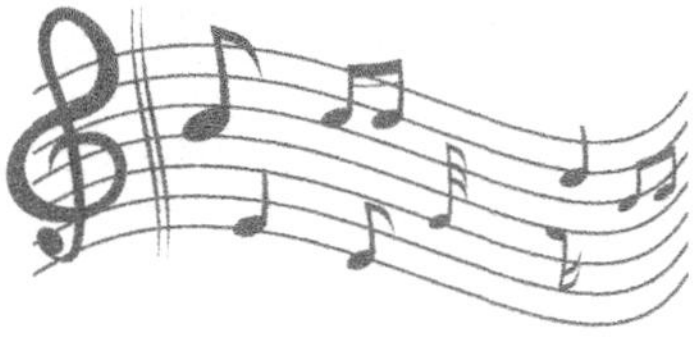

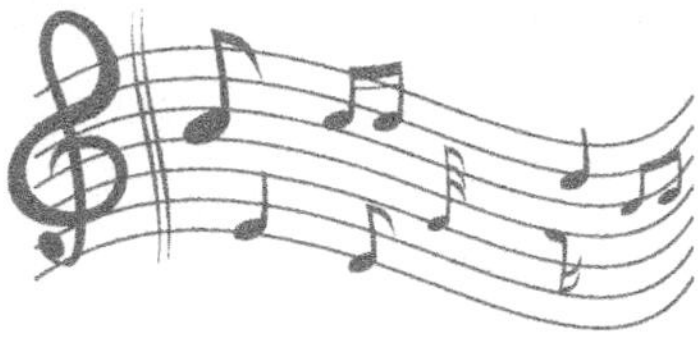

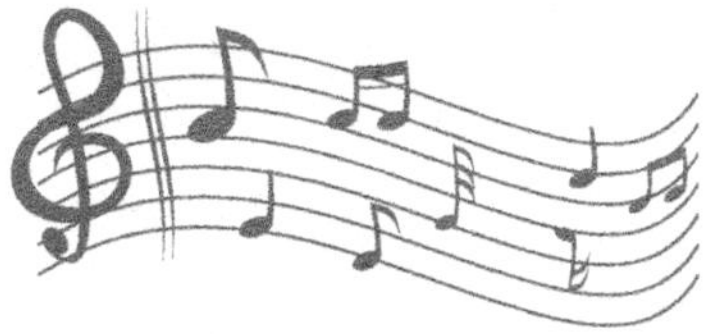

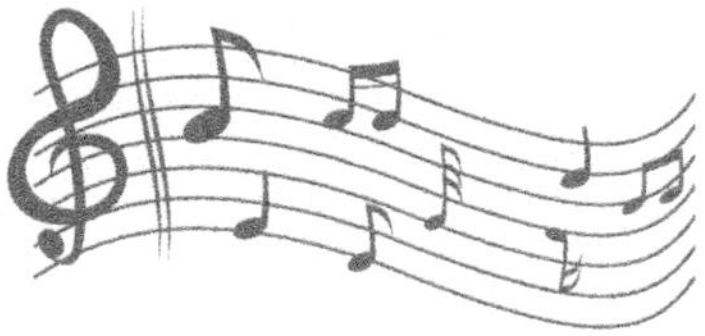

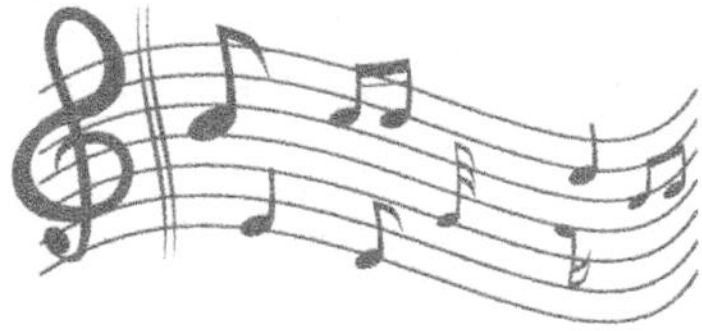

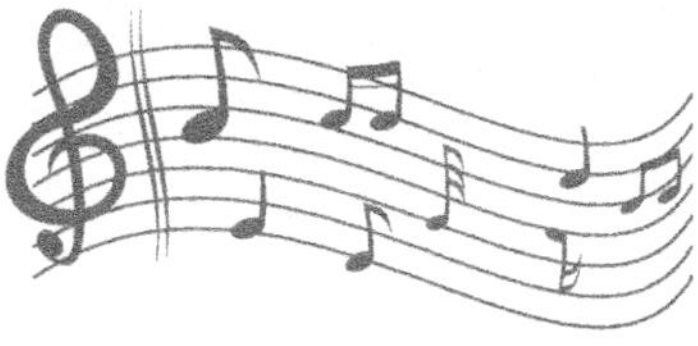

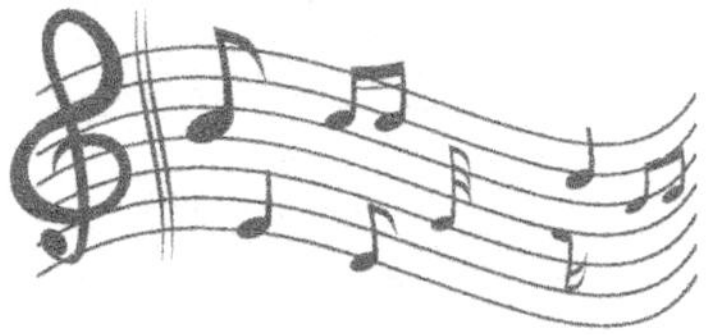

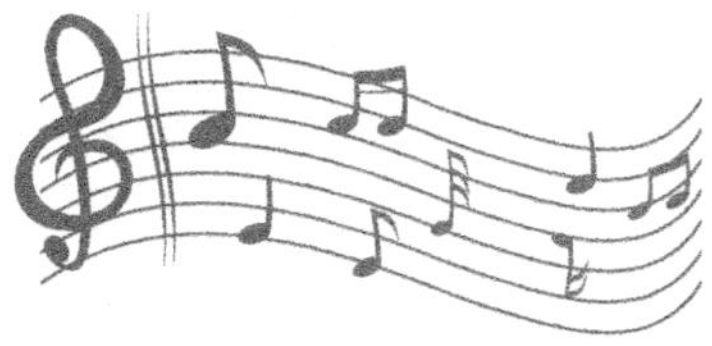

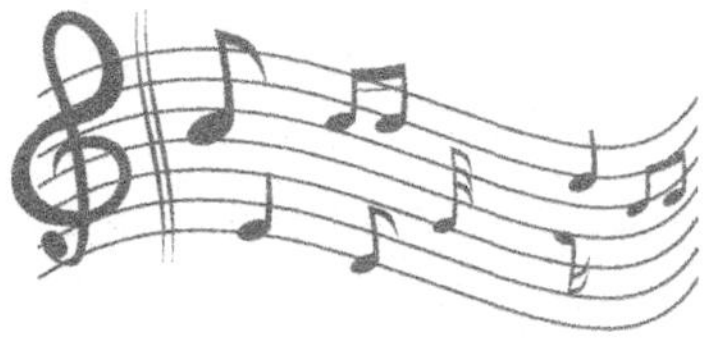

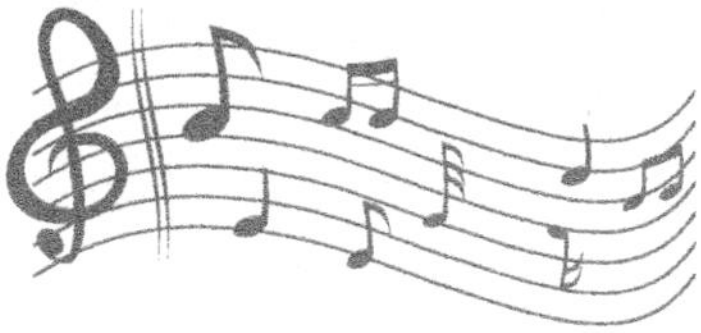

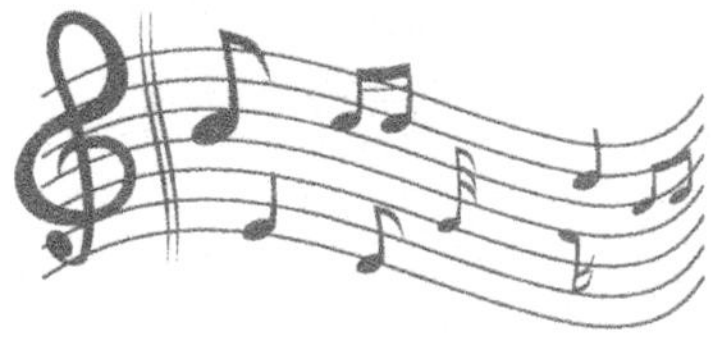

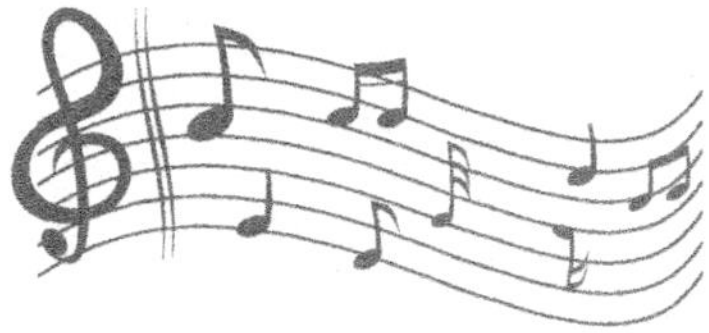

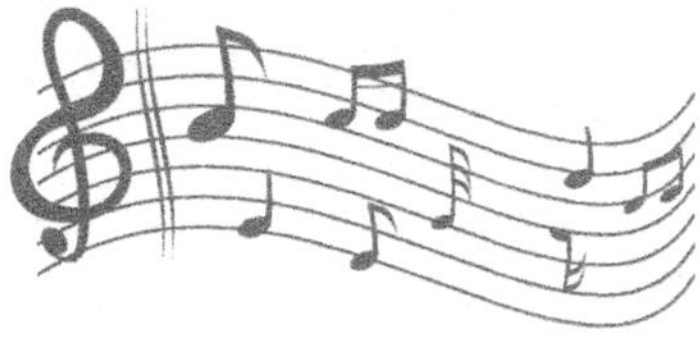

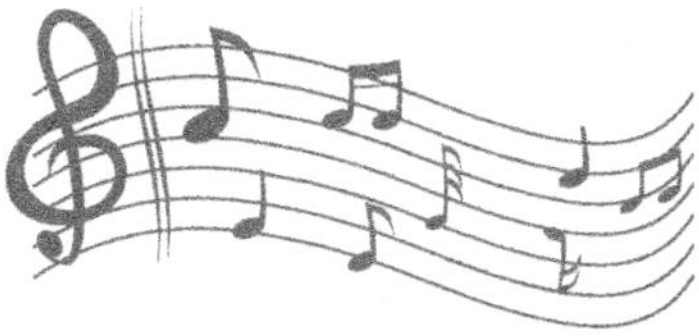

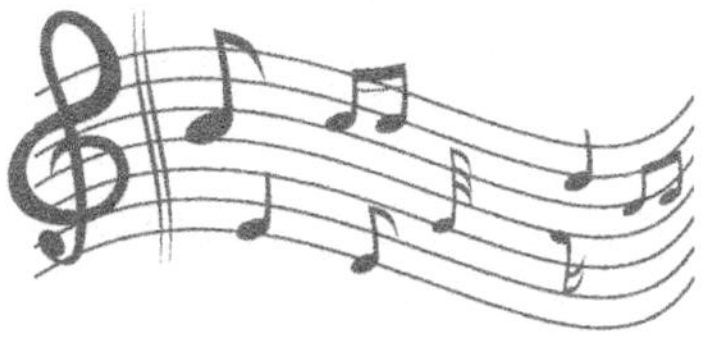

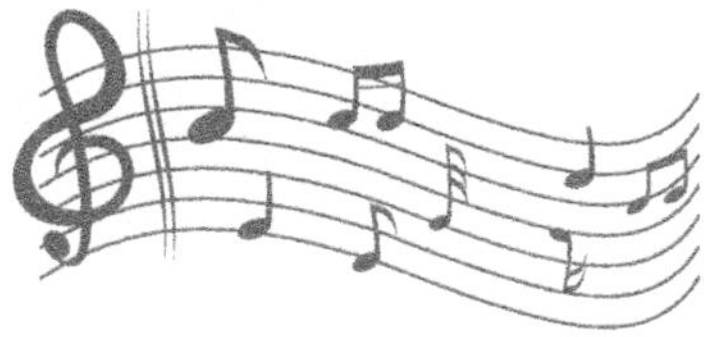

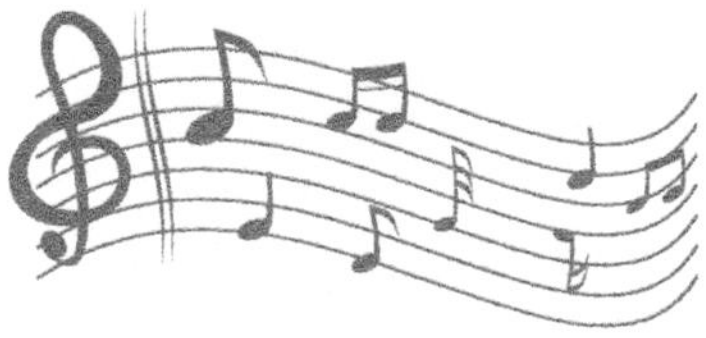

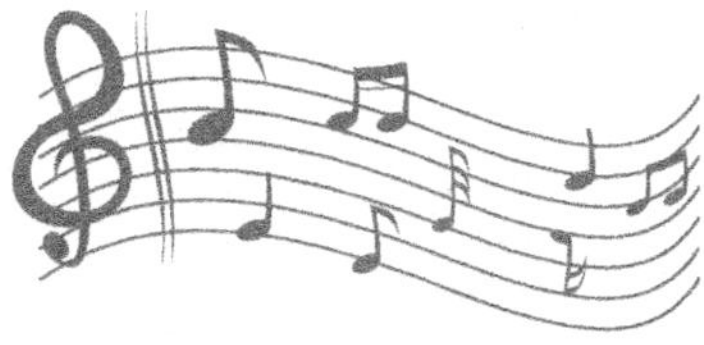

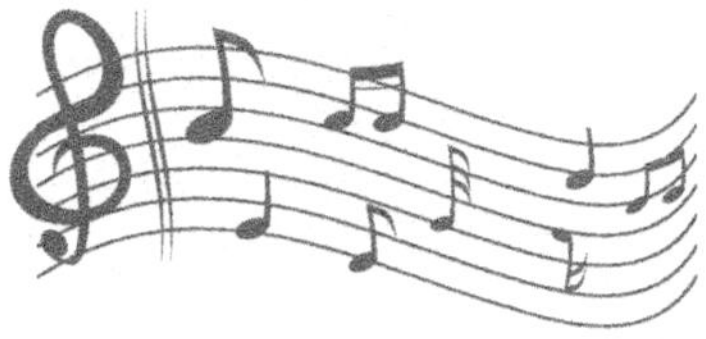

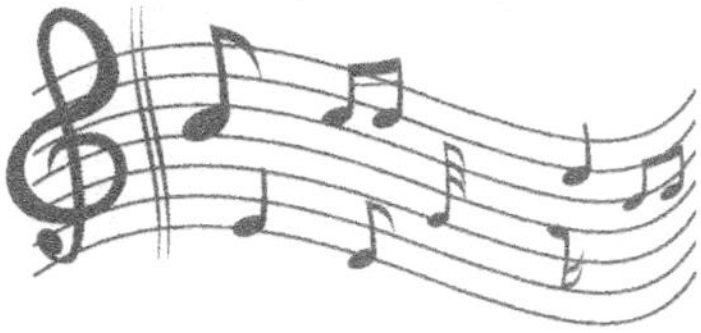

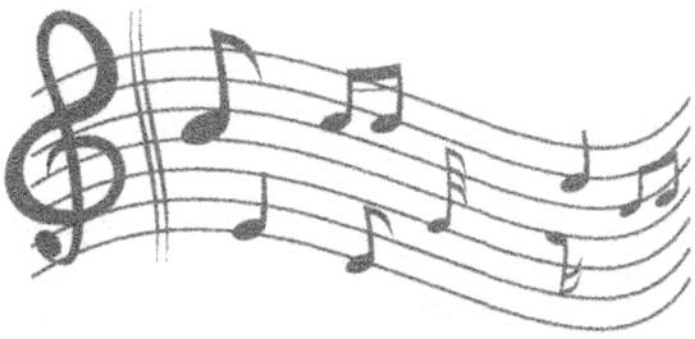

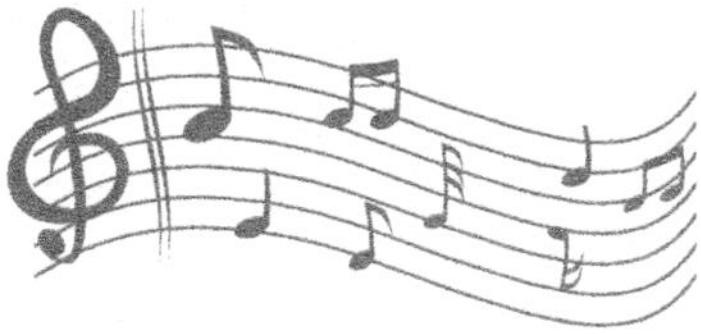

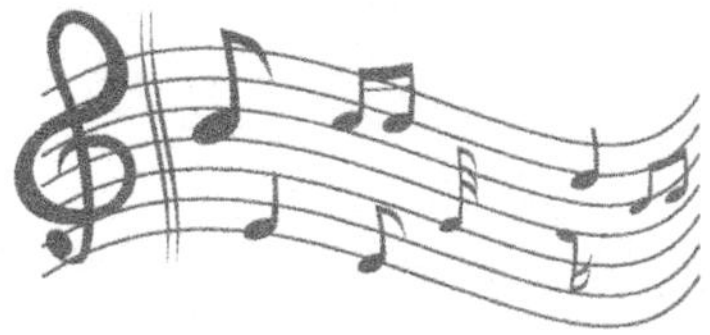

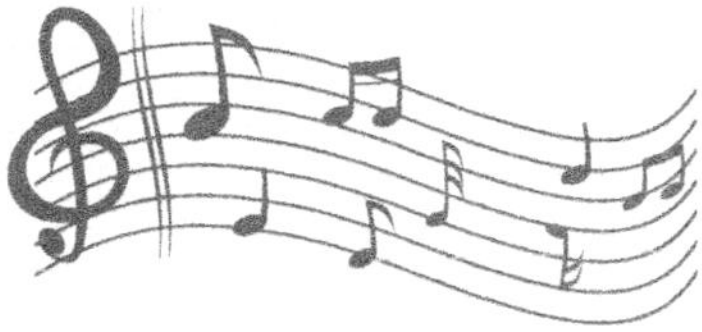

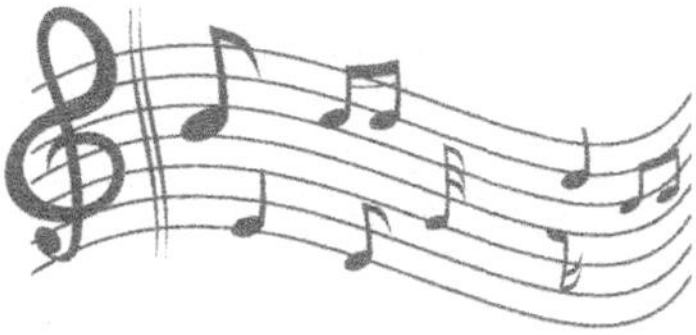

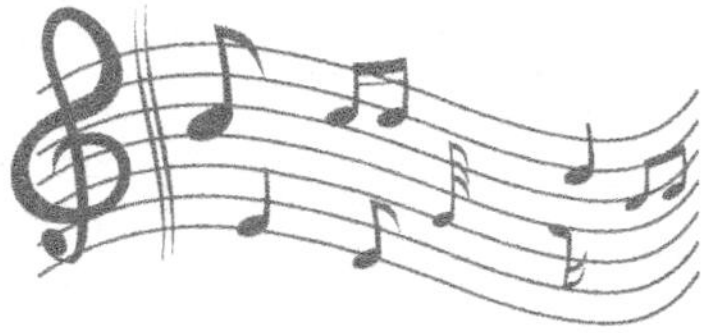

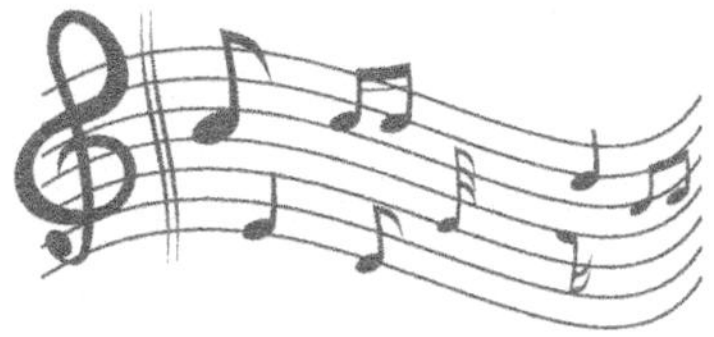

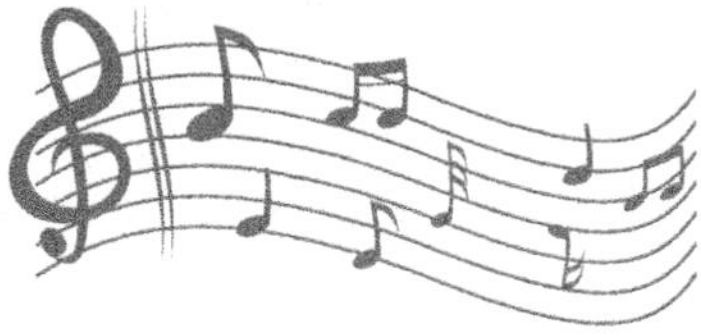

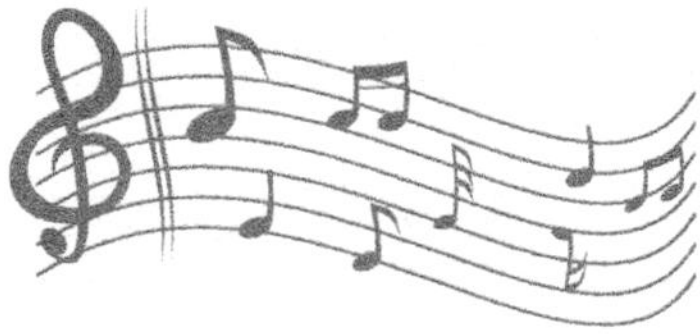

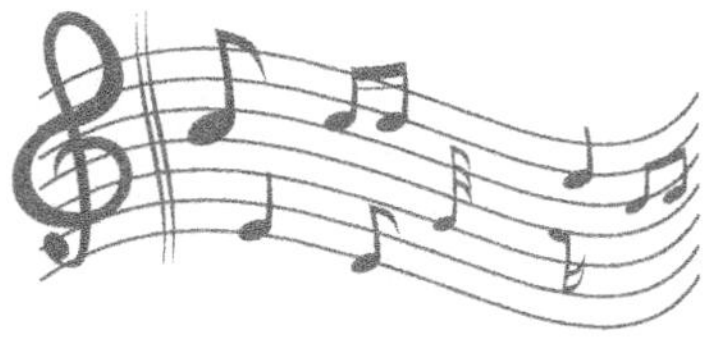

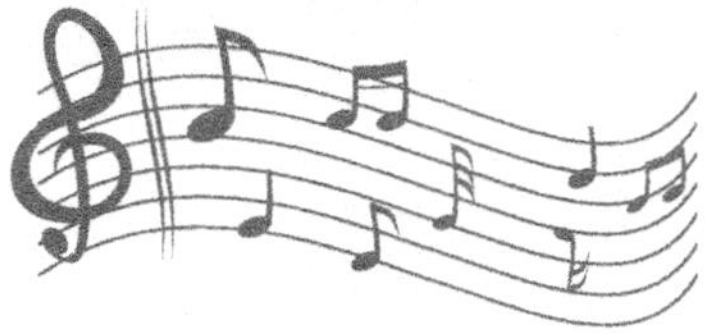

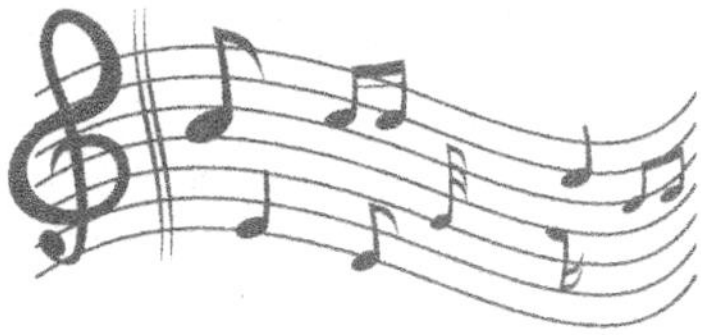

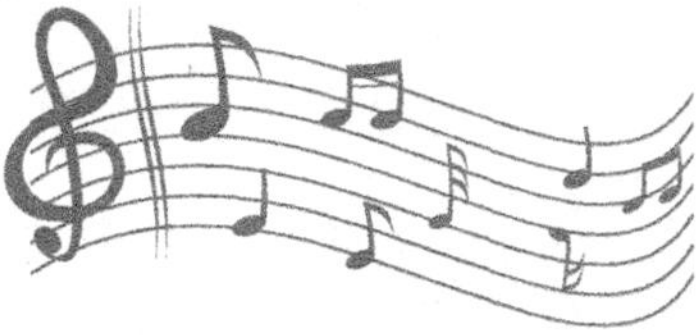

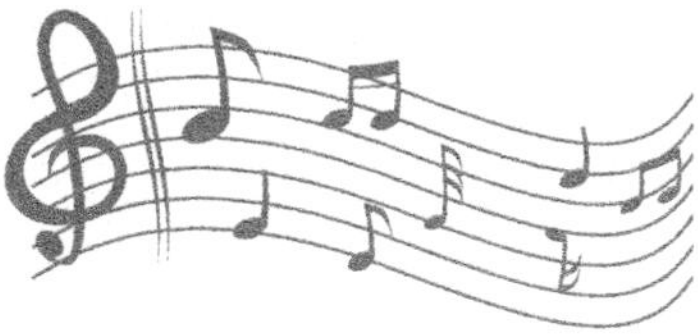

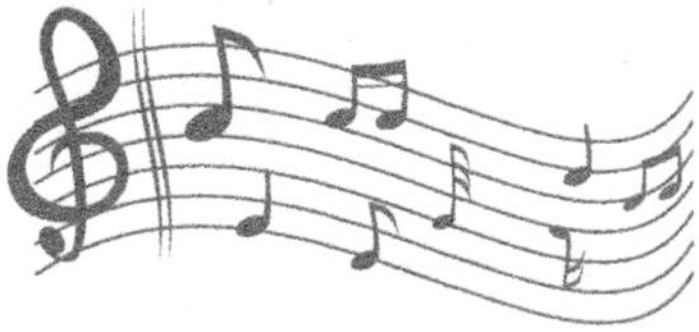

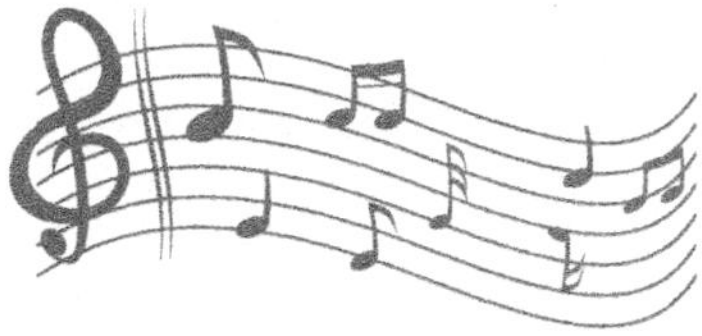

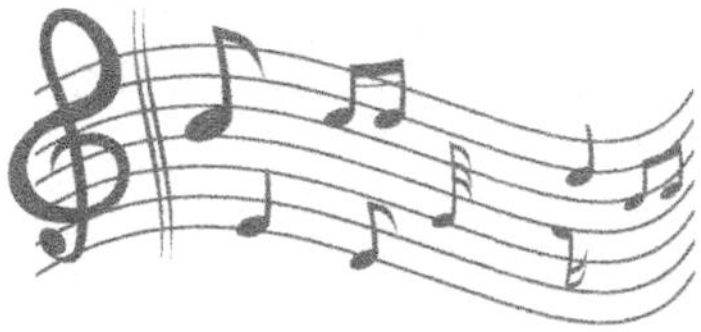

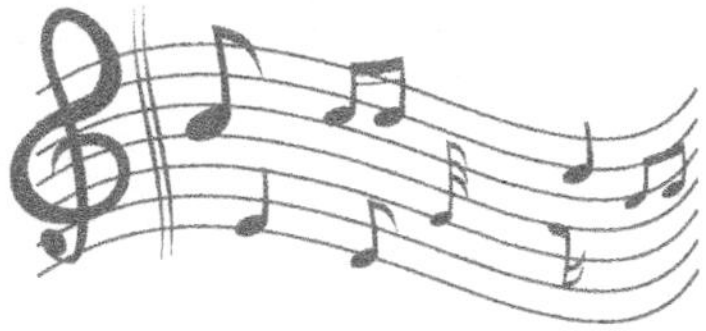

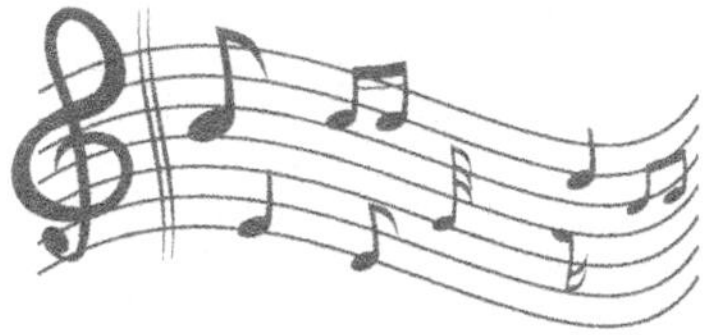

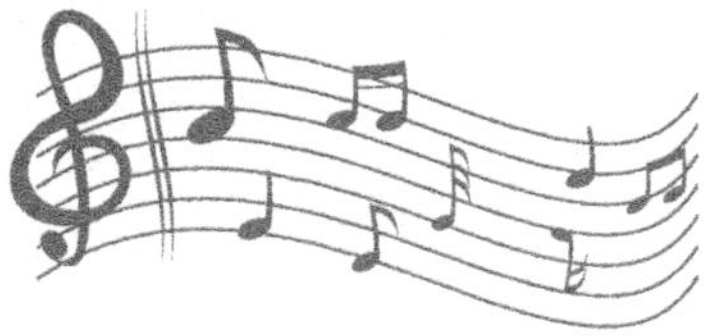

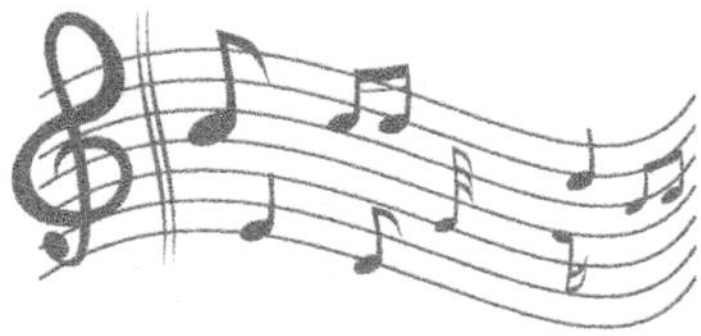

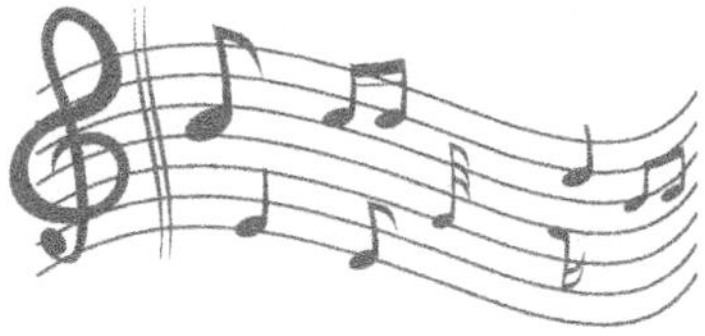

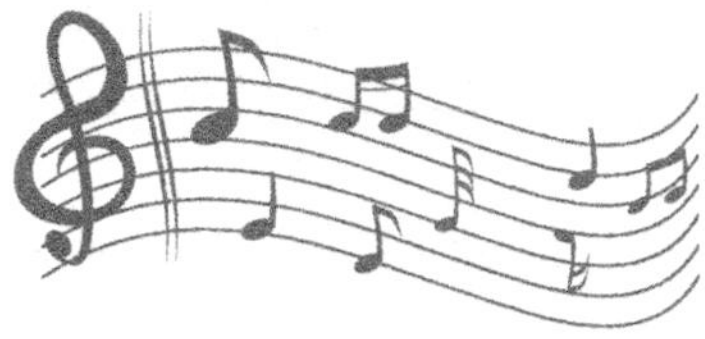

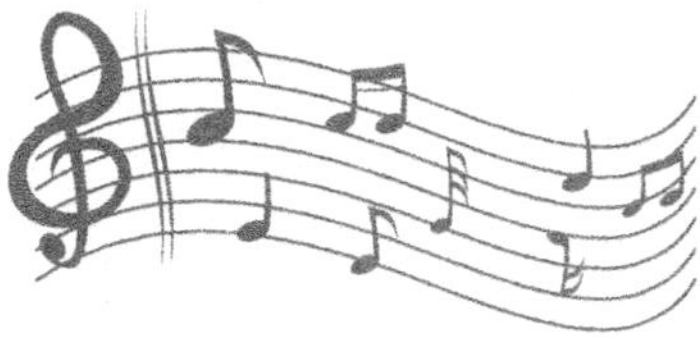

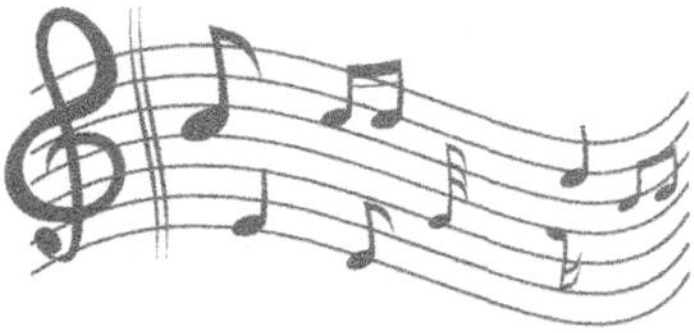

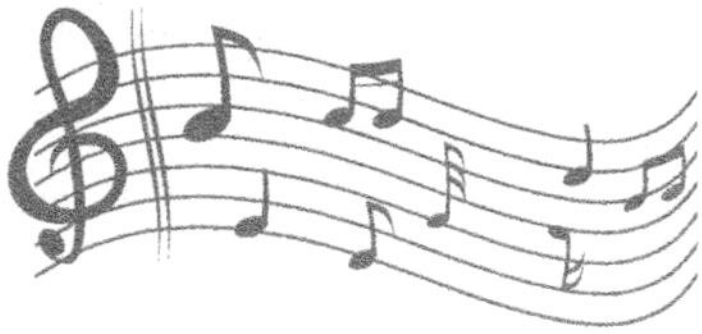

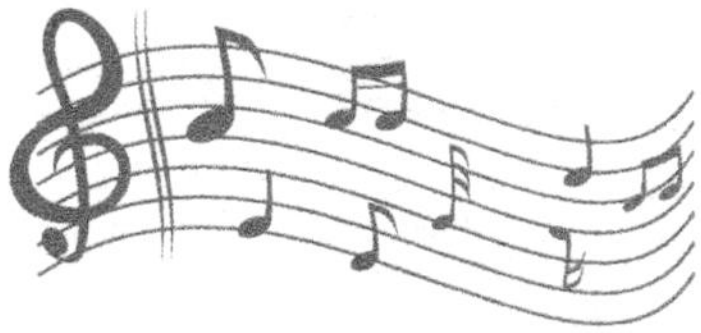

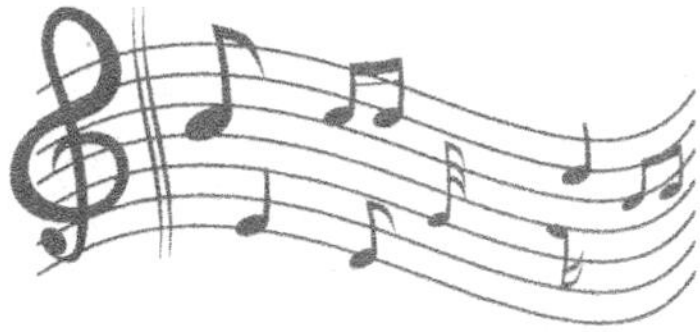

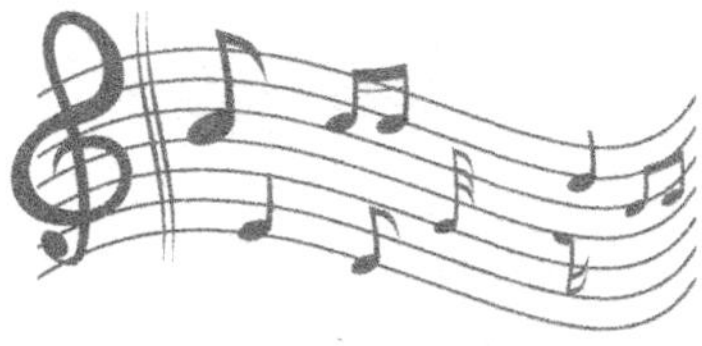

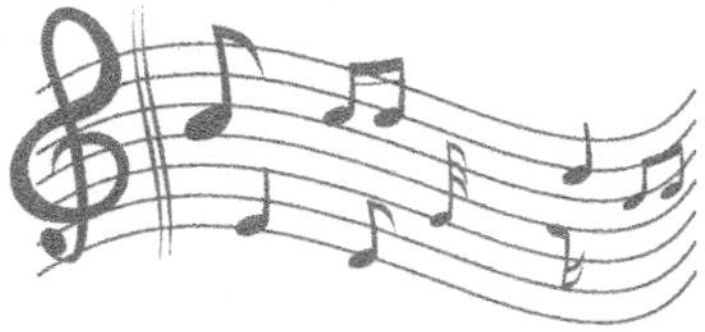

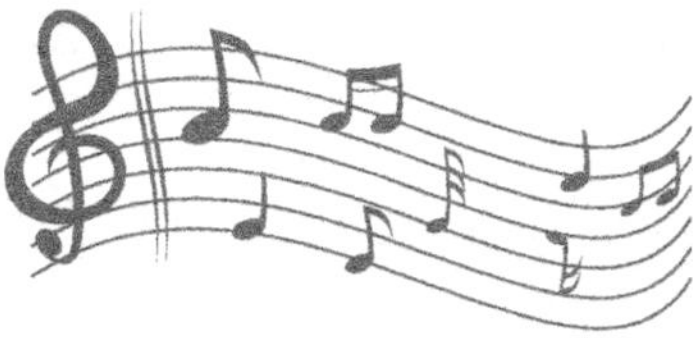

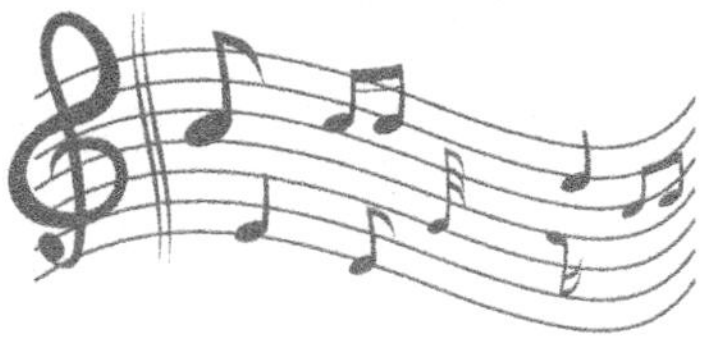

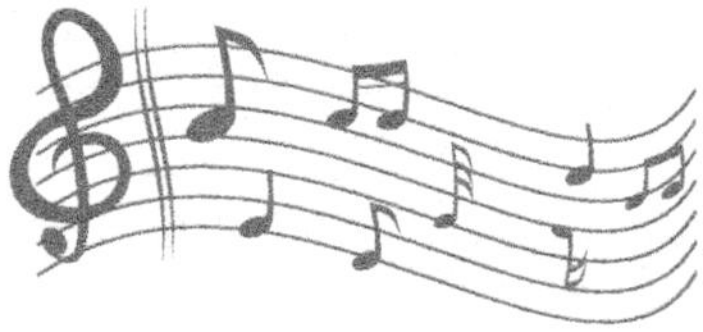

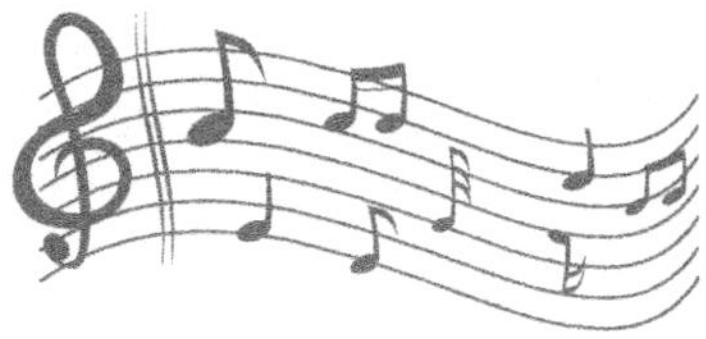

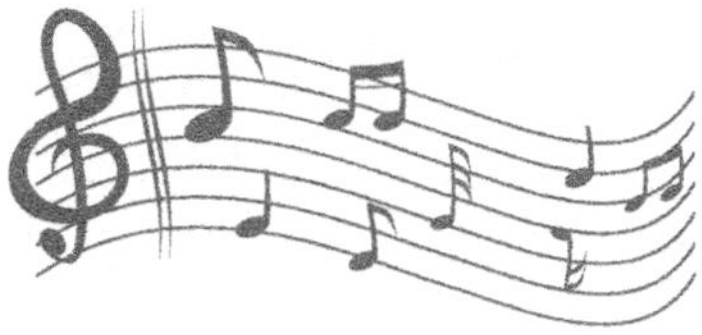

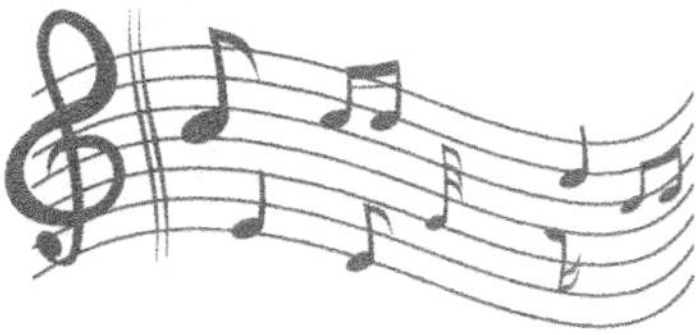

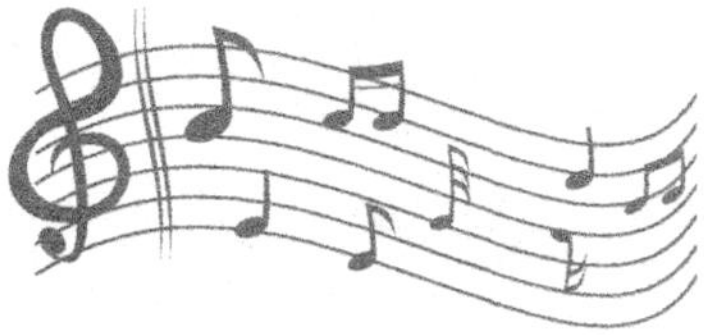

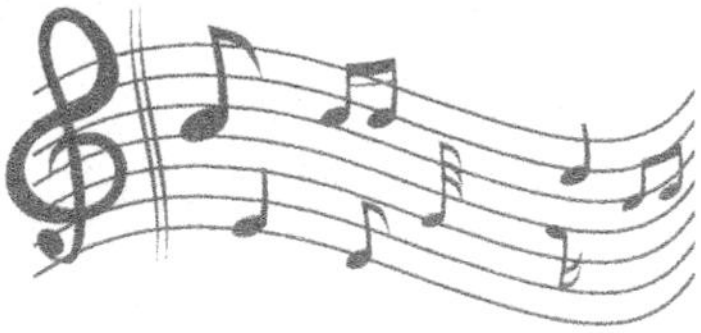

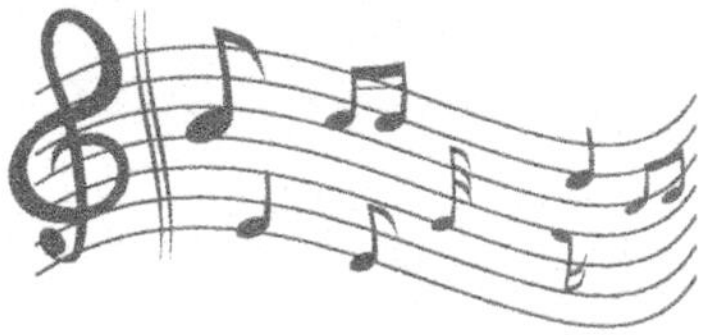

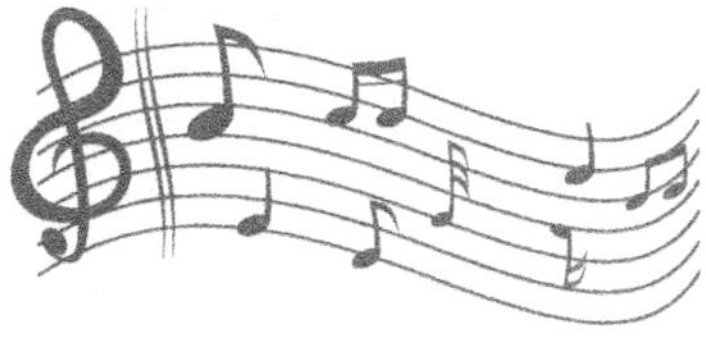

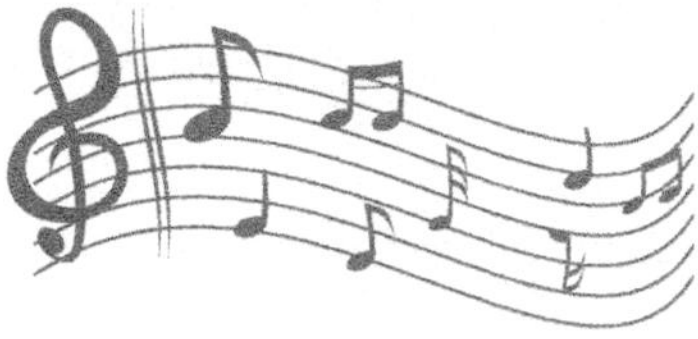

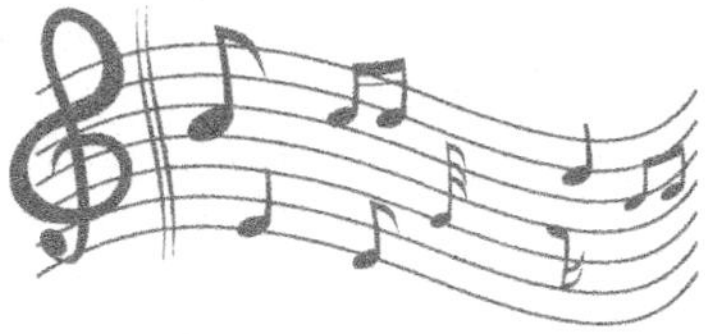

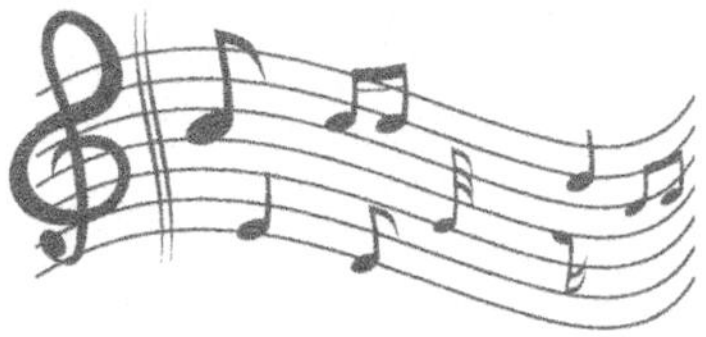

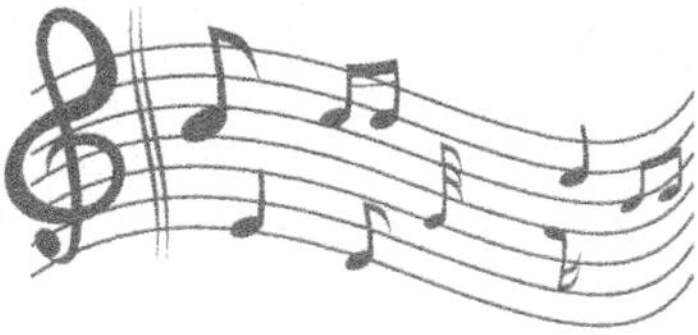

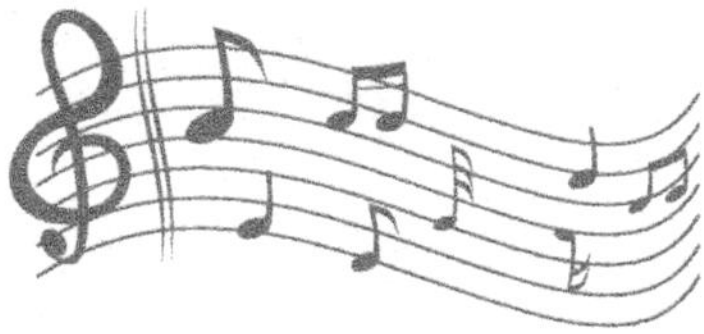

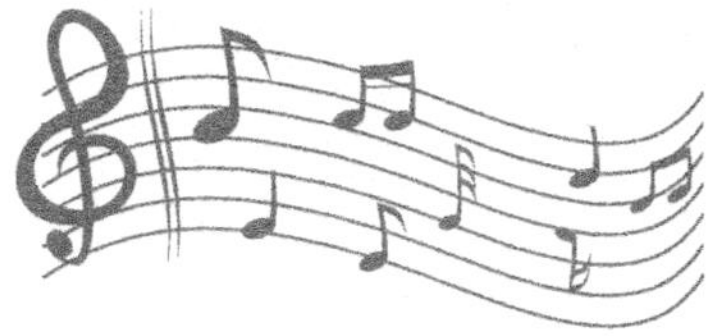

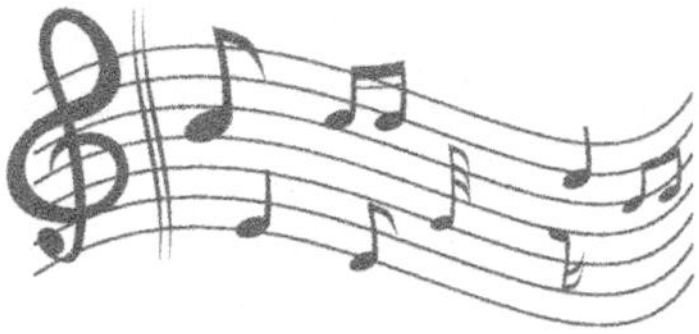

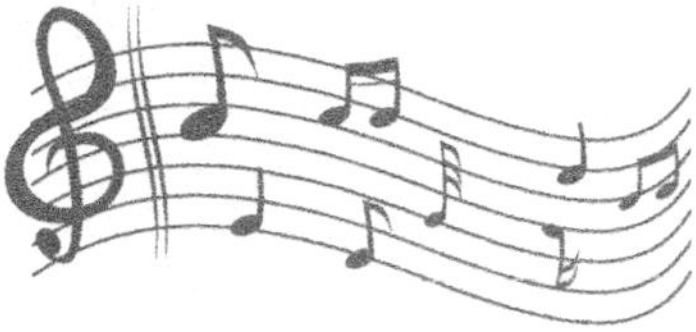

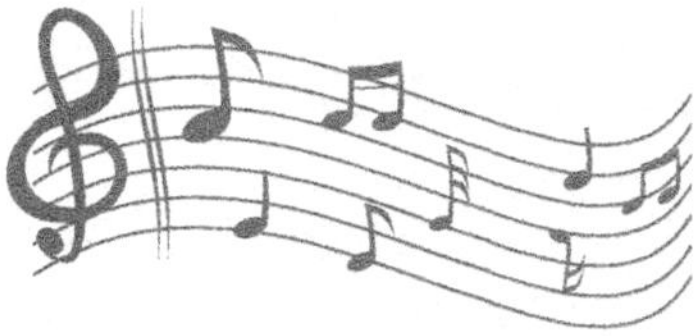

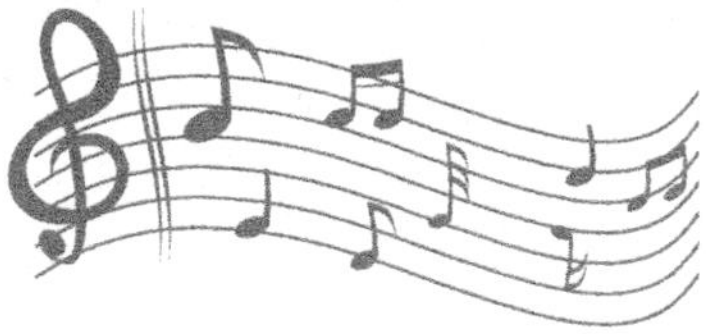

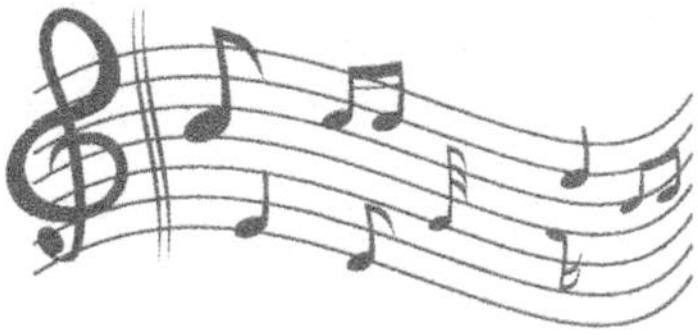

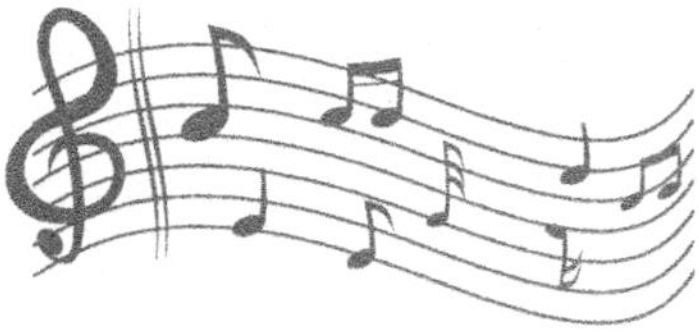

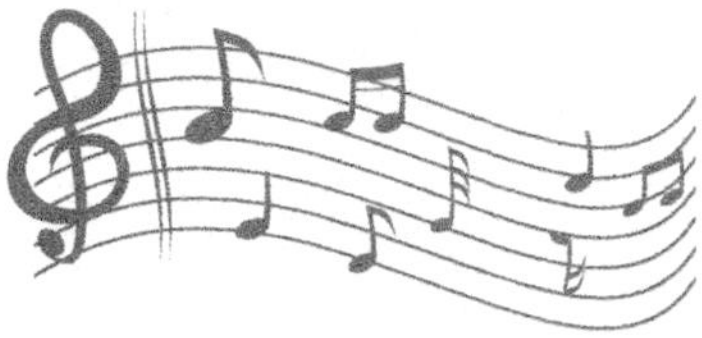

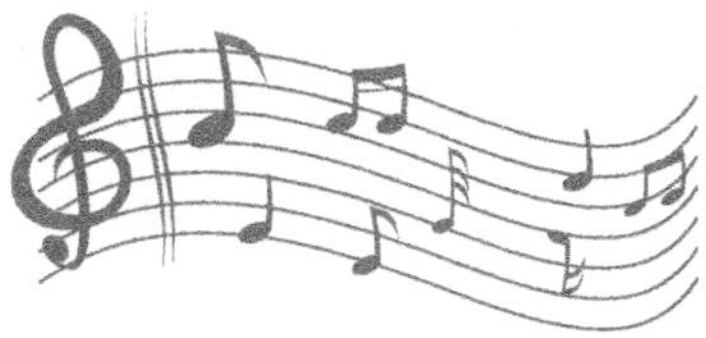

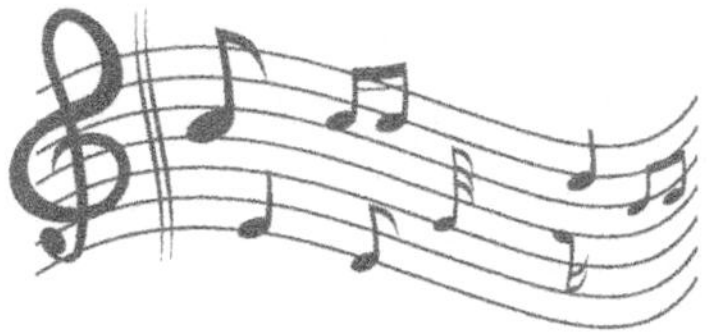

Made in the USA
Middletown, DE
08 June 2023

32301116R00071